Complete Practical Guide on Yam Flour Processing

yam → washing → peeling → wet milling

flour ← dry milling ← drying ← dewatering

By

Benadine Nonye Nduagu

(www.Agric4Profits.com)

Complete Practical Guide on Yam Flour Processing

Yam flour, also known as elubo or pounded yam flour, is a popular food product made from yam tubers. It is widely consumed in West African countries and can be used to make various dishes.

In Summary:

The process of producing yam flour involves several steps, including harvesting the yam, peeling, washing, slicing, parboiling, drying, milling, and packaging.

The description of the yam flour processing line includes:

Yam cleaning and peeling → Yam grinding → Screening and filtering → Sifting → Drying → Fine milling → High-quality yam flour packing.

Yam flour production machine flow process chart.

Yam Flour Production Plant Introduction

To produce high-quality yam flour, the fresh roots must be healthy without rot and well-handled from the farm. The roots should be processed within 24 hours after harvesting.

1. Yam washing and peeling: Before peeling, the raw yam will be washed first to remove the sand, mud, and other impurity. Peeling is essential work for making high-quality yam flour. After washing, the yam will be peeled by the yam peeling machine.

2. Wet milling: The peeled yam will be transported into a clean stainless steel yam milling machine to obtain uniformly smooth mash. The yam mash must be uniformly smooth without lumps. The smoothness of the mash determines the quality, yield, and market value of the finished yam flour.

3. Dewatering: For commercial automatic production, we use the press filter to press the yam mash for removing the water as much as possible.

4. Cake breaking: After pressing, the yam mash will be pressed into the yam cake. The yam cake will be transported into a milling machine for breaking into wet powder form.

5. Drying and sieving: The specially designed yam flour drying machine will dry the wet yam in a few seconds. After drying, the moisture level of yam flour can meet national regulatory standards. Then the yam flour will be sieved to separate the big particle flour.

6. Milling: For getting high-quality yam flour, the dry big particle cassava flour will be milled again by a fine flour mill.

7. Packaging: Pack desired quantities of yam flour in polythene bags, seal or stitch as appropriate. This avoids the absorption of moisture of the flour from the environment.

For more information about the yam flour production plant, yam starch production plant, and all other yam processing machines, please feel free to contact us.

Now let us explain in detail the complete step-by-step guide on how to process yam flour for personal use or commercial purposes:

1. Harvesting

Start by harvesting mature yam tubers. Choose yams that are mature, firm, and free from diseases or pests. Harvesting is typically done when the yam plants have fully grown and the vines have started to dry up.

Commercial yam flour processing involves a systematic approach to harvesting yam tubers to ensure a good yield and quality.

Here is a detailed step-by-step guide on the process of harvesting yam tubers for commercial yam flour processing:

1. Timing: Determine the appropriate time for harvesting yam tubers. The timing may vary depending on the yam variety and local climatic conditions.

Generally, yams are harvested when the vines have started to dry up and turn brown, indicating that the tubers have reached maturity.

2. Prepare harvesting tools: Gather the necessary tools for harvesting, including a sharp machete or harvest knife, gloves, and baskets or crates for collecting the harvested tubers. Ensure that the tools are clean and in good condition.

3. Pre-harvest preparations: Before harvesting, clear the area around the yam plants by removing any weeds or other obstacles. This will make it easier to access the tubers and minimize damage during the harvesting process.

4. Loosening the soil: Use a digging fork or a shovel to loosen the soil around the base of the yam plant. Gently insert the tool into the soil and carefully lift the plant, taking care not to damage the tubers. Loosening the soil helps to facilitate the removal of the tubers.

5. Tubers extraction: Once the soil is loosened, carefully lift the yam plant from the ground, keeping the tubers intact. Shake off excess soil from the tubers and remove any attached vines or roots.

6. Sorting and grading: Inspect the harvested yam tubers for any signs of disease, rot, or damage. Sort the tubers based on size and quality. Select the best-quality tubers for further processing, as damaged or diseased tubers may affect the overall quality of the yam flour.

7. Curing: After sorting, allow the harvested yam tubers to undergo a curing process. Curing helps to improve the shelf life of the tubers and enhances the flavor and texture. Place the tubers in a well-ventilated area with moderate temperature and humidity for about 7-14 days.

8. Storage: Once the curing process is complete, store the yam tubers in a cool and dry place. Use crates or bins to stack the tubers, ensuring proper airflow to prevent mold or rot. Regularly check the stored tubers for any signs of spoilage and remove any affected ones to prevent the spread of diseases.

Proper handling and care during the harvesting process are essential to ensure the quality and yield of the yam tubers for subsequent processing into yam flour.

2. Peeling

Peeling yam tubers is an essential step in commercial yam flour processing. Proper peeling ensures the removal of the outer skin, which can contain dirt, contaminants, or residues that may affect the quality of the final product.

Use a sharp knife or a yam peeler to remove the outer skin of the yam tubers. Ensure that the peeling is thorough to eliminate any dirt or contaminants.

Here is a detailed step-by-step guide on the process of peeling yam tubers in commercial yam flour processing:

1. Sorting: Before peeling, sort the harvested yam tubers based on size and quality. Remove any damaged, diseased, or moldy tubers from the batch, as they may affect the quality of the yam flour.

2. Washing: Thoroughly wash the selected yam tubers in clean water to remove any visible dirt or debris. You can use a brush or a soft cloth to scrub the tubers gently, ensuring that all surfaces are cleaned. This step helps to ensure the cleanliness of the tubers before peeling.

3. Preparation: Set up a clean and sanitized workspace for peeling the yam tubers. Ensure that all peeling tools, such as sharp knives or yam peelers, are clean and in good condition. It is recommended to wear gloves to maintain hygiene and protect your hands.

4. Peeling: Hold a yam tuber firmly in one hand and use a sharp knife or a yam peeler in the other hand to remove the outer skin.

Start from one end of the tuber and work your way toward the other end, applying gentle pressure to remove the skin while minimizing the loss of flesh. Repeat this process for each yam tuber.

5. Trimming: After peeling, inspect the yam tubers for any remaining skin or blemishes. Use a knife to trim off any remaining skin or discoloration, ensuring that the tubers are clean and uniform in appearance.

6. Rinsing: Once all the yam tubers are peeled and trimmed, rinse them again in clean water to remove any loose skin or debris. This step helps to ensure that the peeled yam tubers are free from any contaminants.

7. Drainage: Place the peeled yam tubers on a clean, perforated tray or a drying rack to allow excess water to drain off. It's important to remove as much water as possible before proceeding to the next steps.

8. Further processing: After peeling, the yam tubers are ready for the next stages of yam flour processing, which typically involve slicing, parboiling, drying, milling, and packaging.

The peeled yam tubers can be sliced into thin pieces using a knife or a yam slicer, depending on the desired thickness for drying and milling.

It's important to maintain good hygiene practices throughout the peeling process. Ensure that the workspace, tools, and hands are clean and sanitized. Proper handling and care during peeling contribute to the overall quality and safety of the yam flour produced.

3. Washing

Washing yam tubers is a crucial step in commercial yam flour processing to ensure the removal of dirt, contaminants, and any residues that may affect the quality of the final product.

Thoroughly wash the peeled yam tubers in clean water to remove any remaining dirt or debris. This step helps to ensure the cleanliness of the final product.

Here is a detailed step-by-step guide on the process of washing yam tubers in commercial yam flour processing:

1. Sorting: Before washing, sort the harvested yam tubers based on size and quality. Remove any damaged, diseased, or moldy tubers from the batch, as they may affect the quality of the yam flour.

2. Preparation: Set up a clean and sanitized workspace for washing the yam tubers. Ensure that all washing equipment, such as basins, containers, or sinks, are thoroughly cleaned and free from any residues.

3. Filling the washing area: Fill the washing area, such as a basin or sink, with clean water. The water should be enough to submerge the yam tubers fully.

4. Submerging the tubers: Gently place the sorted yam tubers into the water-filled basin or sink, ensuring that they are fully submerged. Handle the tubers carefully to avoid any bruising or damage.

5. Soaking: Allow the yam tubers to soak in the water for a few minutes. This helps to loosen any dirt or debris attached to the surface of the tubers.

6. Cleaning: Use a brush or a soft cloth to scrub the yam tubers gently, focusing on areas with stubborn dirt or blemishes. Work on the entire surface of each tuber, ensuring thorough cleaning.

7. Rinsing: Once the tubers are cleaned, transfer them to another basin or sink filled with clean water for rinsing. Gently agitate the tubers in the water to remove any loosened dirt or cleaning residue.

8. Repeat if necessary: If the tubers are still not adequately cleaned after the first round of washing and rinsing, repeat steps 4 to 7 until the tubers are clean and free from dirt and contaminants.

9. Final rinse: After the last round of cleaning, transfer the yam tubers to a final basin or sink filled with clean water for a final rinse. Ensure that all residues and dirt are completely removed from the tubers.

10. Drainage: Once the final rinse is complete, place the washed yam tubers on a clean, perforated tray or a drying rack to allow excess water to drain off. It's important to remove as much water as possible before proceeding to the next steps of yam flour processing.

Maintaining good hygiene practices throughout the washing process is crucial. Ensure that the washing area, equipment, and hands are clean and sanitized. Proper handling and care during washing contribute to the overall quality and safety of the yam flour produced.

4. Slicing

Slicing yam tubers is a crucial step in commercial yam flour processing as it prepares the tubers for drying and subsequent milling.

Cut the washed yam tubers into small, uniform slices. The slices should be thin enough to facilitate the drying process. You can use a sharp knife or a yam slicer for this step.

Here is a detailed step-by-step guide on the process of slicing yam tubers in commercial yam flour processing:

1. Sorted Tubers: Begin with a batch of sorted yam tubers that have been washed and peeled. Remove any damaged or diseased tubers to ensure the quality of the final product.

2. Equipment Preparation: Set up a clean and sanitized workspace for slicing the yam tubers. Ensure that all slicing equipment, such as a sharp knife or a yam slicer, is clean and in good condition. Wearing gloves is recommended to maintain hygiene and protect hands.

3. Tubers Orientation: Place a washed and peeled yam tuber on a stable cutting surface. Ensure that the tuber is positioned in a stable and secure manner to avoid accidents or injuries during slicing.

4. Slicing Technique: Use a sharp knife or a yam slicer to cut the yam tuber into thin slices. Slice the tuber uniformly to ensure even drying and milling. The thickness of the slices can vary depending on the desired texture and drying time, but generally, slices around 3-5 mm thick are common for yam flour production.

5. Consistency: Maintain consistent slicing throughout the process to ensure that all yam slices are of similar thickness. This consistency helps in achieving uniform drying and milling results.

6. Repeat: Repeat the slicing process for each yam tuber in the batch. Take care to maintain the quality of the slices by avoiding excessive bruising or damage during slicing.

7. Tubers Preservation: If there is a time gap between slicing and further processing, it's essential to prevent the yam slices from discoloring or drying out. You can place the slices in a container filled with water or cover them with a damp cloth to keep them moist until further processing.

8. Further Processing: After slicing, the yam tuber slices are ready for parboiling, drying, milling, and packaging, as per the specific yam flour processing steps. Each of these subsequent steps will further transform the sliced yam tubers into yam flour.

It's important to maintain good hygiene practices throughout the slicing process. Ensure that the workspace, equipment, and hands are clean and sanitized. Proper handling and care during slicing contribute to the overall quality and safety of the yam flour produced.

5. Parboiling

Parboiling is an essential step in commercial yam flour processing as it helps to reduce the drying time, soften the yam slices, and preserve their color.

Parboiling is an important step that helps to reduce the drying time and preserve the color of the yam slices.

Place the yam slices in a large pot of boiling water and let them cook for about 5-10 minutes. Stir occasionally to ensure even cooking.

Here is a detailed step-by-step guide on the process of parboiling yam tubers in commercial yam flour processing:

1. Sliced Yam Tubers: Start with a batch of yam tubers that have been washed, peeled, and sliced into thin, uniform slices. The slices should be approximately 3-5 mm thick for optimal parboiling.

2. Boiling Water: Fill a large pot with clean water and bring it to a boil. Ensure that there is enough water to fully submerge the yam slices during parboiling.

3. Adding Yam Slices: Carefully add the sliced yam tubers to the boiling water, ensuring that they are fully submerged. Stir gently to prevent the slices from sticking together.

4. Parboiling Time: Allow the yam slices to cook in the boiling water for approximately 5-10 minutes. The exact parboiling time may vary depending on the thickness of the slices and the desired texture. Stir the yam slices occasionally to ensure even cooking.

5. Testing for Parboiling: After the initial parboiling time, test the yam slices for doneness. The slices should be partially cooked, and firm but slightly softened. Insert a fork or a knife into a slice to check its texture. It should offer slight resistance but not be fully cooked or mushy.

6. Draining: Once the yam slices are partially cooked, carefully drain the hot water from the pot using a colander or a sieve. Remove the yam slices from the pot and transfer them to a clean container or a cooling rack.

7. Cooling: Allow the parboiled yam slices to cool down completely. This step helps to halt the cooking process and prepare the slices for further processing.

8. Preservation: If there is a time gap between parboiling and further processing, it's important to prevent the yam slices from discoloring or drying out. You can place the slices in a container with water or cover them with a damp cloth to keep them moist until further processing.

The parboiled yam slices are now ready for the subsequent steps in yam flour processing, such as drying, milling, and packaging. The parboiling process enhances the efficiency of the drying process and improves the quality of the final yam flour product.

It's important to maintain good hygiene practices throughout the parboiling process. Ensure that the equipment, containers, and hands are clean and sanitized. Proper handling and care during parboiling contribute to the overall quality and safety of the yam flour produced.

6. Cooling

After parboiling, drain the hot water from the pot and transfer the yam slices to a clean container or a cooling rack. Allow them to cool down completely before proceeding to the next step.

Cooling is important to halt the cooking process and prepare the yam slices for drying, milling, or other subsequent steps.

Here is a detailed step-by-step guide on the process of cooling yam tubers in commercial yam flour processing:

1. Parboiled Yam Slices: Begin with a batch of yam slices that have been parboiled until they are partially cooked. These slices would have been drained from the hot water after the parboiling process.

2. Arrangement for Cooling: Transfer the parboiled yam slices to a clean container or a cooling rack. Arrange them in a single layer to allow for proper airflow and even cooling. If necessary, use multiple containers or racks to accommodate all the yam slices without overcrowding.

3. Spacing: Ensure that there is enough space between the yam slices to prevent them from sticking together as they cool. This spacing helps maintain the quality and individuality of each slice.

4. Natural Cooling: Allow the parboiled yam slices to cool down naturally at room temperature. This process typically takes anywhere from 30 minutes to a few hours, depending on the ambient temperature and the thickness of the slices.

5. Avoid Contamination: During the cooling process, make sure to protect the yam slices from any potential sources of contamination. Keep them away from dirt, dust, insects, or any other foreign particles that may affect their quality.

6. Moisture Control: To prevent the yam slices from drying out or becoming dehydrated during the cooling process, cover the container or racks with a clean, breathable cloth or plastic wrap. This covering helps retain moisture and maintains the optimal texture of the parboiled yam slices.

7. Check for Complete Cooling: After a sufficient cooling period, check the yam slices for complete coolness. They should no longer emit heat and should be at or near room temperature throughout. The slices should also have a firm texture and should not feel warm to the touch.

Once the yam slices are completely cooled, they are ready for the subsequent steps in yam flour processing, such as drying, milling, or packaging. The cooling process helps prepare the yam slices for these subsequent stages and ensures optimal results in terms of flavor, texture, and quality.

Maintaining good hygiene practices throughout the cooling process is crucial. Ensure that the containers, cooling racks, and covering materials are clean and sanitized. Proper handling and care during cooling contribute to the overall quality and safety of the yam flour produced.

7. Drying

Drying yam tubers is an essential step in commercial yam flour processing. It helps to preserve the tubers and remove moisture, ensuring the production of high-quality yam flour.

There are different methods you can use for drying the yam slices. The traditional method involves spreading the slices on clean, flat surfaces, such as mats or trays, and placing them under the sun to dry. This process may take several days, depending on the weather conditions.

Alternatively, you can use mechanical dryers or ovens to speed up the drying process. If using a mechanical dryer, set the temperature to around 50-60°C (122-140°F) and place the yam slices on the drying trays. Stir or turn the slices occasionally for even drying.

There are several methods of drying, including sun drying, mechanical drying, or a combination of both. Choose the most suitable method based on your available resources and scale of production.

Drying yam tubers is a crucial step in commercial yam flour processing as it removes moisture from the parboiled slices and prepares them for milling into flour. Proper drying ensures the preservation and quality of the yam flour.

Here is a detailed step-by-step guide on the process of drying yam tubers in commercial yam flour processing:

1. Sun Drying: In this method, the trays or racks containing the yam slices are placed in a well-ventilated area under direct sunlight. The slices are periodically turned to ensure uniform drying.

Sun drying may take several days to complete, depending on the weather conditions and the desired moisture content.

2. Mechanical Drying: Commercial yam flour processing often utilizes mechanical dryers to accelerate the drying process and ensure consistency. These dryers can be heated air dryers, tray dryers, or belt dryers.

The yam slices are placed on trays or a conveyor belt and exposed to heated air, which removes moisture from the slices. The temperature and drying time are carefully controlled to prevent over-drying or under-drying.

3. Spacing: Ensure that there is adequate spacing between the yam slices during drying. This allows for proper air circulation and uniform drying. Avoid overcrowding the slices, as it can lead to uneven drying and potential spoilage.

4. Turning or Flipping: If sun drying, periodically turn or flip the yam slices to ensure even exposure to sunlight. If using a mechanical dryer, follow the recommended instructions for turning or flipping the slices, if necessary.

5. Drying Duration: The drying time for yam slices can vary depending on various factors such as slice thickness, ambient temperature, humidity, and drying method.

Sun drying may take several days or more, while mechanical drying can be faster, typically within a few hours to a day. Monitor the slices regularly to determine their dryness level.

6. Dryness Testing: To assess the dryness of the yam slices, take a few samples and check their texture and moisture content. The slices should be completely dry, brittle, and break easily when bent. They should not feel soft or have any moisture content.

7. Moisture Content: It's crucial to ensure that the yam slices reach an appropriate moisture content for safe storage and milling into flour. Aim for a moisture content of around 12-14% for optimal yam flour production. Use a moisture meter or consult with experts to determine the moisture content.

8. Cooling: Once the yam slices are completely dry, allow them to cool down to room temperature before further processing. This helps prevent moisture condensation during milling or packaging.

9. Storage: Store the dried yam slices in clean, airtight containers or bags to maintain their quality. Label the containers with necessary information such as the product name, date of drying, and any relevant details.

Proper hygiene practices should be followed throughout the drying process. Ensure that the drying surfaces, equipment, and containers are clean and sanitized. Good handling and care during drying contribute to the overall quality and safety of the yam flour produced.

8. Milling

Once the yam slices are completely dried and brittle, it's time to grind them into a fine powder. Use a hammer mill or a commercial milling machine to achieve the desired consistency. The milled yam flour should be smooth and free from lumps.

Milling yam tubers is a critical step in commercial yam flour processing as it transforms the dried yam slices into a fine powder form. Milling helps to achieve the desired texture and consistency of the yam flour.

Here is a detailed step-by-step guide on the process of milling yam tubers in commercial yam flour processing:

1. Dried Yam Slices: Begin with a batch of dried yam slices that have been properly dried and cooled down. The yam slices should be brittle and have a moisture content of around 12-14%.

2. Milling Equipment: Set up a clean and sanitized milling area with appropriate equipment. For commercial yam flour processing, you will need a hammer mill or a commercial milling machine. Ensure that the milling equipment is in good working condition and clean.

3. Preparing the Mill: Follow the manufacturer's instructions for setting up and adjusting the milling equipment. Ensure that the machine is properly calibrated for the desired fineness of the yam flour.

4. Batch Size: Determine the appropriate batch size for milling based on the capacity of the milling machine and the volume of yam slices you are processing. Start with a manageable batch size to ensure efficient milling and control over the process.

5. Loading the Mill: Carefully feed the dried yam slices into the hopper or feeding mechanism of the milling machine. Feed the slices slowly and in a controlled manner to prevent overloading or jamming of the machine.

6. Milling Process: Turn on the milling machine and allow it to operate, grinding the yam slices into a fine powder. The machine will crush and pulverize the yam slices, reducing them to the desired particle size.

7. Sieving: Once the yam slices have been milled, pass the resulting powder through a fine mesh sieve. This step helps to remove any coarse particles or fibers, ensuring a smooth and uniform texture for the yam flour.

8. Repeat Milling: If necessary, repeat the milling process for any remaining batches of dried yam slices until all the slices are milled into flour. Ensure that the milling machine is properly cleaned and sanitized between batches to avoid contamination.

9. Quality Control: Conduct quality control checks throughout the milling process to ensure the yam flour meets the desired standards. Assess the texture, color, and fineness of the flour to ensure consistency and quality.

10. Packaging: Transfer the milled yam flour into clean, airtight containers or bags for packaging. Label the packages with necessary information such as the product name, date of milling, and any relevant details.

Proper hygiene practices should be followed throughout the milling process. Ensure that the milling equipment, sieves, containers, and hands are clean and sanitized.

Good handling and care during milling contribute to the overall quality and safety of the yam flour produced.

9. Sieving

Sieving yam flour is a critical step in commercial yam flour processing as it helps to achieve a smooth and uniform texture by removing any coarse particles or fibers.

Pass the milled yam flour through a fine mesh sieve to remove any remaining coarse particles or fibers. This step helps to achieve a uniform texture and improve the overall quality of the flour.

Here is a detailed step-by-step guide on the process of sieving yam flour in commercial yam flour processing:

1. Milled Yam Flour: Begin with a batch of milled yam flour that has been produced from dried and milled yam slices. The yam flour should be in a powdered form.

2. Sieving Equipment: Set up a clean and sanitized area for sieving the yam flour. You will need a fine mesh sieve or a sifter. Ensure that the sieve is clean and in good condition.

3. Sieve Size: Choose a sieve with an appropriate mesh size to achieve the desired texture for the yam flour. The mesh size should be fine enough to remove any coarse particles or fibers while allowing the fine flour to pass through.

4. Batch Size: Determine the appropriate batch size for sieving based on the capacity of the sieve and the volume of yam flour you are processing. Start with a manageable batch size to ensure efficient sieving and control over the process.

5. Loading the Sieve: Place the sieve over a clean container or a receptacle that can catch the sifted yam flour. Carefully pour a portion of the milled yam flour onto the sieve, ensuring that it does not overflow.

6. Sieving Process: Gently shake or tap the sieve to sift the yam flour through the mesh. Use a spoon or a soft brush to help agitate the flour and assist in the sieving process. This will help separate the fine flour from any remaining coarse particles or fibers.

7. Coarse Particles Removal: As you sift the yam flour, periodically check the sieve for any accumulation of coarse particles or fibers. Remove these particles from the sieve to maintain an efficient sieving process.

8. Repeat Sieving: If necessary, repeat the sieving process for any remaining batches of yam flour until all the flour is sieved. Ensure that the sieve is properly cleaned and sanitized between batches to avoid contamination.

9. Quality Control: Conduct quality control checks throughout the sieving process to ensure the yam flour meets the desired standards. Assess the texture, fineness, and uniformity of the sifted flour to ensure consistent and high-quality yam flour.

10. Packaging: Transfer the sifted yam flour into clean, airtight containers or bags for packaging. Label the packages with necessary information such as the product name, date of sieving, and any relevant details.

Proper hygiene practices should be followed throughout the sieving process. Ensure that the sieving equipment, containers, and hands are clean and sanitized. Good handling and care during sieving contribute to the overall quality and safety of the yam flour produced.

10. Proper Packaging

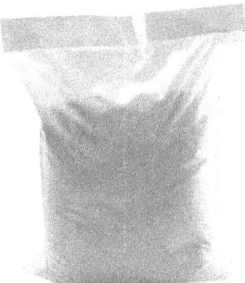

Proper packaging is essential in commercial yam flour processing to ensure the freshness, quality, and safety of the final product.

Finally, package the yam flour in airtight containers or bags to maintain its freshness and prevent moisture absorption. Label the packages with the necessary information, such as the product name, date of production, and any relevant nutritional facts.

Here is a detailed step-by-step guide on the process of properly packaging yam flour in commercial yam flour processing:

1. Prepared Yam Flour: Begin with a batch of yam flour that has been milled, sieved, and is ready for packaging. The yam flour should be smooth, free from lumps, and of high quality.

2. Packaging Materials: Choose appropriate packaging materials that are clean, food-grade, and provide airtight seals. Common packaging options include plastic bags, laminated pouches, or food-grade containers.

3. Packaging Size: Determine the appropriate packaging size based on market demand, product shelf life, and production capacity. Consider packaging options such as small retail-sized packages or bulk packaging for commercial customers.

4. Packaging Process: Follow these steps to properly package yam flour:

a. Clean and Sanitize: Ensure that all packaging materials and equipment are thoroughly cleaned and sanitized before use. This helps maintain the hygiene and integrity of the yam flour.

b. Fill the Packages: Fill each packaging unit with the appropriate amount of yam flour. Use measuring tools or weigh scales to ensure accurate portioning. Avoid overfilling or underfilling the packages.

c. Sealing: Seal the packaging units using appropriate sealing methods. This can include heat sealing, zip-lock closures, or adhesive seals, depending on the packaging materials used. Ensure that the seals are tight and airtight to prevent moisture and air from entering.

d. Labeling: Attach labels to the packaged yam flour units. Include essential information such as the product name, production date, batch number, weight or volume, nutritional information, storage instructions, and any required regulatory labeling.

e. Quality Control: Conduct quality checks during the packaging process to ensure that each unit of yam flour meets the desired standards. Inspect for any packaging defects, foreign particles, or signs of spoilage.

5. Storage: Store the packaged yam flour in a cool, dry place away from direct sunlight and other sources of heat. Proper storage conditions help maintain the quality, flavor, and shelf life of the yam flour.

6. Distribution: Prepare the packaged yam flour for distribution. Arrange for appropriate transportation and storage during transit to ensure that the yam flour reaches consumers or retailers in optimal condition.

7. Quality Assurance: Implement quality control measures throughout the packaging process. This can include regular testing for moisture content, microbial safety, and shelf stability to ensure compliance with food safety standards.

Proper hygiene practices should be followed throughout the packaging process. Ensure that the packaging area, equipment, and hands are clean and sanitized. Good handling and care during packaging contribute to the overall quality and safety of the yam flour produced.

11. Quality Control

Conduct quality control checks throughout the processing to ensure the yam flour meets the desired standards. This can involve testing for moisture content, color, texture, and microbial safety.

Quality control is a crucial aspect of commercial yam flour processing to ensure that the final product meets the desired standards in terms of safety, flavor, texture, and shelf life.

Here is a detailed step-by-step guide on the process of quality control in commercial yam flour processing:

1. Establish Quality Parameters: Determine the specific quality parameters that need to be monitored and controlled throughout the processing of yam flour. These parameters may include moisture content, color, texture, microbial safety, and any other relevant quality attributes.

2. Sampling Plan: Develop a sampling plan to collect representative samples at various stages of the yam flour processing. The sampling plan should identify the sampling locations, frequency, and sample sizes required for each quality parameter.

3. Sample Collection: Collect samples according to the established sampling plan. Ensure that the samples are taken from different batches or lots to account for potential variations in the raw materials or processing conditions.

4. Laboratory Testing: Send the collected samples to a reputable laboratory equipped with appropriate testing facilities. Perform the necessary tests to assess the quality attributes of the yam flour.

These tests may include moisture analysis, color measurement, texture analysis, and microbial testing.

5. Interpretation of Test Results: Receive the test results from the laboratory and interpret them based on the established quality standards.

Compare the results to the predefined acceptable ranges for each quality parameter. Identify any deviations or non-conformities that need to be addressed.

6. Corrective Actions: If the test results indicate any quality issues or non-conformities, implement appropriate corrective actions.

This may involve adjusting processing parameters, improving sanitation practices, or addressing any identified weaknesses in the processing system.

7. Documentation: Maintain proper documentation of all quality control activities, including test results, corrective actions taken, and any relevant observations. This documentation serves as a record of quality assurance efforts and can be used for future reference or audits.

8. Ongoing Monitoring: Continuously monitor the processing conditions, equipment, and personnel involved in yam flour production. Regularly collect samples and conduct in-house quality tests to ensure that the established quality standards are consistently met.

9. Regulatory Compliance: Ensure that the yam flour processing facility complies with relevant food safety regulations and industry standards. Stay updated on any changes in regulations and adjust the quality control processes accordingly.

10. Staff Training: Provide regular training to the staff involved in yam flour processing on quality control procedures, good manufacturing practices, and hygiene protocols. Well-trained personnel play a vital role in maintaining consistent quality throughout the processing.

11. Continuous Improvement: Seek opportunities for continuous improvement in the yam flour processing operations.

Regularly review the quality control processes, seek feedback from customers, and explore innovative technologies or practices to enhance the quality of the final product.

By following these steps, you can establish a robust quality control system in commercial yam flour processing, ensuring that the yam flour meets the desired quality standards and satisfies customer expectations.

12. Proper Storage

Proper storage of yam tubers is crucial in commercial yam flour processing to maintain their quality, prevent spoilage, and extend their shelf life.

Store the packaged yam flour in a cool, dry place to prolong its shelf life. Proper storage conditions are essential to maintain the quality of the flour over time.

It's important to note that commercial yam flour processing requires proper hygiene practices and adherence to food safety standards. Ensure that all equipment and utensils used are clean and sanitized.

Additionally, follow good manufacturing practices and comply with relevant regulations to ensure the production of safe and high-quality yam flour. Store the finished yam flour in a cool, dry place to prolong its shelf life.

Here is a detailed step-by-step guide on the process of storing yam tubers in commercial yam flour processing:

1. Sorting: Before storage, sort the yam tubers based on size, quality, and any visible signs of damage or disease. Remove any damaged or diseased tubers from the batch, as they can affect the overall storage conditions and quality of the yam flour produced.

2. Cleaning: Thoroughly clean the yam tubers to remove any dirt, debris, or residues. Use a soft brush or a cloth to gently scrub the surface of the tubers. Proper cleaning helps prevent the transfer of contaminants during storage.

3. Drying: Ensure that the yam tubers are properly dried before storage. Excess moisture can lead to rotting or the growth of mold and bacteria. Allow the tubers to air dry in a well-ventilated area until the surface is dry to the touch.

4. Storage Conditions: Select an appropriate storage area for the yam tubers. The ideal conditions for yam storage include a cool, dry, and well-ventilated environment.

The temperature should be around 12-15°C (54-59°F), and the relative humidity should be maintained between 65% and 70%.

5. Storage Containers: Choose suitable storage containers or bins for the yam tubers. These containers should be clean, food-grade, and well-ventilated to allow for airflow and prevent condensation. Avoid using containers made of materials that may cause off-flavors or chemical reactions.

6. Arrange Tubers: Place the yam tubers in the storage containers in a single layer, without overcrowding. Avoid stacking the tubers too high, as this can cause damage or compress the tubers, leading to spoilage. Leave enough space between the tubers to allow for airflow.

7. Regular Inspection: Regularly inspect the stored yam tubers for any signs of spoilage, rot, or disease. Remove any affected tubers immediately to prevent the spread of spoilage to other tubers.

8. Temperature and Humidity Control: Monitor the storage area's temperature and humidity levels regularly. Make necessary adjustments to maintain the recommended conditions. Consider using fans or dehumidifiers if needed.

9. Air Circulation: Ensure adequate air circulation in the storage area. This helps prevent the buildup of moisture and the growth of mold or bacteria. Arrange the storage containers in a way that allows for proper airflow around the tubers.

10. Pest Control: Implement appropriate pest control measures to prevent infestation by insects or rodents. Regularly inspect the storage area for signs of pests and take necessary actions to eliminate them.

11. Rotation: Practice proper rotation of the stored yam tubers. Use the "first in, first out" principle, where the oldest tubers are used or sold first, to ensure freshness and minimize wastage.

12. Documentation: Maintain records of the storage conditions, including temperature, humidity, and any observations or actions taken. This documentation can be helpful for future reference or audits.

By following these steps, you can ensure the proper storage of yam tubers in commercial yam flour processing, thereby preserving their quality and extending their shelf life.

www.ingramcontent.com/pod-product-compliance
Lightning Source LLC
Chambersburg PA
CBHW072229290526
45794CB00007B/2947